Love Letters to God

LYNN D. MORRISSEY
Artwork by KATIA ANDREEVA

Multnomah Gifts®
Multnomah® Publishers *Sisters, Oregon*

Dedication:

With devotion to the Lord—
Soli Deo Gloria!

With gratitude to my mother, Fern Ayers Morrissey,
for her gifts of love—for me, for the Lord, and for language. Thank you for
your poet's heart and for always believing in me and my writing dream.

In remembrance of Francis (Frank) Joseph Schindler (1945–2003),
for playing the music of life with grace, dignity, and passion to the end.

Love Letters to God

© 2004 by Lynn D. Morrissey
published by Multnomah Gifts®, a division of Multnomah® Publishers, Inc. P.O. Box 1720, Sisters, Oregon 97759

Artwork by Katia Andreeva is reproduced under license from Koechel Peterson & Associates., Inc. and may not be reproduced without permission. For further information regarding art prints featured in this book, please contact: Koechel Peterson & Associates, Inc., 2600 East 26th Street, Minneapolis, Minnesota, 55406, 1-612-721-5017.

International Standard Book Number: 1-59052-189-7

Design by Koechel Peterson & Associates., Inc., Minneapolis, Minnesota

Unless otherwise indicated, Scripture quotations are taken from:
The Holy Bible, New International Version (NIV) ©1973, 1984 by International Bible Society, used by permission of Zondervan Publishing House; *The Living Bible* (TLB) ©1971. Used by permission of Tyndale House Publishers, Inc. All rights reserved. *New American Standard Bible* (NASB) © 1960, 1977 by the Lockman Foundation; *The Holy Bible*, New King James Version (NKJV) ©1984 by Thomas Nelson, Inc. *The New Testament in Modern English, Revised Edition* (PHILLIPS) ©1958, 1960, 1972 by J. B. Phillips

Multnomah Publishers, Inc., has made every effort to provide proper and accurate source attribution for all selections used in this book. Should any attribution be found to be incorrect, the publisher welcomes written documentation supporting correction for subsequent printings. We gratefully acknowledge the cooperation of other publishers and individuals who have granted permission for use of their material.

Multnomah is a trademark of Multnomah Publishers, Inc., and is registered in the U.S. Patent and Trademark Office. The colophon is a trademark of Multnomah Publishers, Inc.

Printed in Belgium

For Information:
MULTNOMAH PUBLISHERS, INC. • P.O. BOX 1720 • SISTERS, OR 97759

Library of Congress Cataloging-in-Publication Data

Morrissey, Lynn D.
  Love letters to god / by Lynn D. Morrissey.
    p. cm.
Includes bibliographical references.
  ISBN 1-59052-189-7 (Hardcover)
  1. Christian women–Religious life. 2. Spiritual journals. I. Title.

BV4527.M66 2004
248.4′6–dc22
                          2003017002

Contact Lynn Morrisey at words@brick.net.

04 05 06 07 08 09—10 9 8 7 6 5 4 3 2 1 0

Table of Contents

Introduction

What cannot letters inspire?
They have souls; they can speak;
they have in them all that force
which expresses the
transports of the heart;
they have all the
fire of our passions.

HÉLOÏSE (1098–1164)

*I*T'S A RAINY DAY. I had planned to spend a quiet afternoon at home, but I sense God's familiar voice beckoning. He whispers softly to my heart, *Come away. Come away with Me.* There are no sweeter words, no sweeter invitation. I can't resist! There is nothing I would rather do than spend time with the One who deeply loves me. So I gather my journal and pen and head for one of our most delightful trysting retreats.

What a perfect afternoon for a rendezvous with God! As I nestle into a cozy corner at my favorite bookstore-café, I gaze out gleaming plate-glass windows. Tissue-paper clouds veil a silver sky. Raindrops dance on the pavement outside while a Vivaldi concerto cavorts over speakers inside.

I sip English tea and, with great anticipation, place my new journal on the table before me. Unknown to the book-lovers reading or buzzing about me, when I open my journal, I am continuing the romance of a lifetime. I'm ready to write another love letter to the living, loving God! I can hardly wait to fill page after page with prayer after prayer—with praises and thanksgiving, pleadings and petitions, confessions and commitments, questions and answers, dreams and longings. Though my journal is yet empty, I know it has hardly enough room to contain the love I want to express to God because of His measureless love for me—hardly enough room to contain the gratitude I owe Him for transforming my life through His gift of written prayer.

I can all too easily remember a time when my life was just as empty as these blank journal pages. As a young woman I was tormented by suicidal depression. I was paralyzed by debilitating shyness and consuming self-hatred. I felt inferior to others, convinced I had nothing to offer. I was also jealous of them because they were everything I yearned to be. My life seemed purposeless, so I drowned my envy, my anger, my confusion, my despair in alcohol.

I wanted to cry out to God in my pain, but I couldn't. Though I loved Him, I never talked to Him because I didn't know how. I found it impossible to verbalize my deep-seated fears and complex emotions. I felt intimidated by the eloquent prayers of my pastors and the expressive prayers of my friends. I also found it difficult to concentrate. I could barely focus for even minutes at a time, and my petitions to God seemed to trail off into oblivion, unfinished, unexpressed. So I stopped praying altogether and wondered whether my life would ever change or if I'd ever feel close to the Lord. The distance between us seemed unbridgeable, and I found the silence to be unbearable.

Then an incident occurred that changed my relationship with God forever. A vengeful woman at work began telling lies to my boss in an effort to get me fired. In order to cope, I began to vent my fear and frustration on paper. The more I wrote, the better I felt. Yet something much more remarkable happened. Without purposely trying, I began crying out to God, asking for His help in this desperate situation. Without even realizing it, I was *praying!* No longer inhibited by formal language, I wrote in my own words about my real-life crisis. No longer groping for words to express how I felt, I focused my thoughts in writing with surprising ease.

I was so excited about communicating with God that I awoke early every morning to meet Him alone in our secret place on the front porch. I wrote my prayers—what I call my love letters to God—in a journal, sometimes for hours at a time. This phenomenon was nothing short of miraculous. I, who had stopped praying, now *couldn't stop* praying! And when I said "I love You, Lord" *in writing,* I felt truly close to Him for the very first time. I was completely aware of His presence. God had joined me on the porch. He was real. He was loving. And He was listening.

As I passionately sought God, He gave me remarkable calm at work until my trial there ended. As I confided in Him daily, His peace consumed my depression, His love gave me significance, and His power gave me victory over drinking. I am convinced that had I not *written* to God, I never would have prayed to Him. Written prayer is the key to my consistent conversation with the Lover of my soul. It is an intimacy that I can enjoy anytime, anyplace. I simply open my journal, lift my pen, and pour out my heart.

I have found that there is something extraordinary about *writing* that frees me to express my emotions and thoughts like no other form of prayer can. Writing an actual letter to God releases me from formality by encouraging my honest conversation with Someone I love, with Someone who loves me.

When I write from my heart, in my own words, in my own way, about what I am feeling and experiencing, I never run out of things to say. And I love that writing naturally slows me down, allowing me more time to talk with and listen to God.

My investment has been worth every second, because the more time I spend with God, the closer He and I become. By praying to God in my journal for over twenty-five years, I have enjoyed a loving relationship with Him. He has allowed me the awesome privilege of knowing Him, and He has helped me discover my purpose, experience my passion, answer my questions, appreciate my blessings, and express my praises. And unlike my verbal prayers—which I soon forget— my written prayers have become a permanent place for exploring my soul, a tangible testimony of God's love and faithfulness in my life, and a detailed document of my spiritual journey.

As you read about how God has used the power of prayer-journaling to change me, I pray that He will use my journey to touch your heart and show you how He could transform your life in amazing ways through His gift of written prayer. You will read about my experiences of doubt and faith, questions and assurances, bitterness and blessing, depression and healing. For in the end, each and every love letter I write leads me straight to the heart of God, where I can experience the depths of His love—His perfect love that makes me whole.

God loves you, too, with unfathomable love—love wider than the sea and higher than the sky. Even the universe cannot contain the extent of His love for you. And though God's love is infinitely vast, it is extraordinarily personal. He has given it to you in the embrace of His crucified Son. He has written it to you in a love letter, His magnified Word.

And you can embrace the Lord with *your* written words. As you pen love letters to God in your journal, you can touch the hem of the garment of His love—the garment of His intimate presence. And in His presence there is fullness of joy!

It is this gift of joy I long for you to know—joy in your prayer-journaling and joy in your journey. You will experience joy as, pen in hand, you travel life's path with the Lover of your soul, recording your steps prayer by prayer in your journal.

God holds out His hand to you and whispers tenderly,

Come away with Me,
    My precious one.
Come away with Me
    so I may tell you
    how much I love you,
    so I may fill your heart with joy.

Will you take this incredible journey with the Lord? Oh, how He eagerly longs for you to! And when you do, your life will never be the same....

My lover spoke
and said to me,
"Arise, my darling,
my beautiful one,
and come with me."

SONG OF SONGS 2:10

Love Letters to God

Letters
mingle souls.

JOHN DONNE

AT OUR ANNUAL CHRISTMAS luncheon, Mother pulled a small envelope from her purse and wordlessly, tenderly presented it to me. I recognized the uneven penmanship as my father's. My mind raced. "Oh, Mother! Is this *the* letter—the one I've begged him to write for so long?" Her glimmering tears answered silently. She suggested I read it when I was alone.

Later that night, as I sat in the hearthroom amid the glow of flickering flames and the hazy halo of Christmas lights, I tore open the envelope with trembling fingers and read the precious missive. Onto several little note pages, my father's stoic soul had melted, giving way to a litany of love. For as long as I could remember, Daddy had never voiced his tenderness toward me. What he could not say in person now flowed freely from his pen. I read and wept—and wept again. Gently placing the papers back in the envelope, I knew I was placing a lifetime of Daddy's love in my heart.

How well I understood my father's awkwardness. I had often tried unsuccessfully to verbalize my love to my heavenly Father. Self-conscious and stilted, I found it impossible to speak my love in prayer. It was difficult to concentrate and to articulate my deepest feelings for God. My endearments were spoken scattershot—blurted erratically, thrown haphazardly to the wind. I began to realize that sentiments so treasured, so tender, must be carefully weighed and thoughtfully considered, mined like gems from the heart's depths.

Then one day I took the time to write a letter to God. It was amazing! My emotions poured forth, spilling over from my heart's reservoir of love. Somehow the very act of writing—this praying on paper—had released a geyser of feelings formerly unexpressed.

Yet this experience really should have come as no surprise. After all, God, our supreme Lover, our great Romancer, knew that a wonderful way to woo His beloved and express His emotions was through a love letter, the Bible. He knew that "letters mingle souls," and

He gave us His heart-print in ink so that we would have the joy of reading, pondering, and tracing its testimony over and over again. Because the spoken word is ephemeral, God bestowed us with a lasting testament of His passion.

God took great pleasure in giving us His written love letter. And we can assume He would also take great delight in receiving our written response. Because God is a writer, it is only natural that we, created in His image, are writers also.

As one author declared, "Love always wants to proclaim itself, to write itself everywhere: in the sand, in the fire, with flowers, in the wind." David, the psalmist and king, knew this. He declared, "My heart is overflowing with a beautiful thought! I will write a lovely poem to the King, for I am as full of words as the speediest writer pouring out his story." When David's psalms were put on paper, the abundance of his heart naturally spilled over into a collection of love letters, the Psalms—the book of Scripture many of us treasure most.

Oh, how we cherish love letters! We wait breathlessly to receive them. We read and reread them. We sprinkle them with perfume, tie them with a satin ribbon, and store them in a gorgeous box. We savor them because they make us feel extraordinary—because someone thought enough of us to write to us, because someone took the time and effort to reveal his inmost, passionate thoughts, because someone trusted us with the greatest gift of all, his heart.

It is the gift of your whole heart that God most desires—a heart without pretense or posturing; a heart in all its honesty, beauty, passion, and brokenness; a heart pulsing with love, joy, sadness, delight, doubt, pain, anguish, even anger. True love expresses *all* emotions, and true love—God's true love for you—accepts them.

The most beautiful way I have found in which to wrap the gift of my heart is within a letter. Love letters are "our heart on our sleeve, our battle standard, our essence, our indelible signature, our emotional fingerprint, our private well of memory...our true secret self."

It is our hidden self we most long to reveal. My love letters reveal my truest essence—my soul made visible in all its intimacy and intricacy. I cannot help but love God because He loves me; I cannot help but write to God because He has written to me. I take the time to write because my Lover is worthy of my efforts. I write because, though physically unseen, God is real, and writing draws me closer to Him. I write because I desire to offer Him more than a hurried "I love You" on the run. I write because I long to embroider my passion with a flourish of my pen, an embellishment of my heart. I write because my spoken sentiments are evanescent, and I desire a permanent way to preserve my thoughts. I write because God values my prayers so much that He says He sprinkles them with incense and saves them in the "golden bowls of heaven."

My ups, my downs, my victories, my defeats, my adoration, my apathy, my faith, my doubts, my questions—and God's responses—are recorded in my journals. These entries are love letters from my heart to God's—messages from His heart to mine—letters sent special delivery to and from heaven that have changed my life on earth. I sign my letters in ink that will one day fade. But God signs His in indelible ink—the blood of His Son shed for me, blood that covers my imperfection and allows me to pray openly to Him.

You show that you are a letter from Christ...written not with ink but with the Spirit of the living God, not on tablets of stone but on tablets of human hearts.

2 CORINTHIANS 3:3

Secret Garden of the Soul

I WALKED IN THE BACK DOOR, my arms encircling a breathtaking bouquet of bearded irises, a frilly profusion of purple and periwinkle. Not having been endowed with green-thumbed grace, I was proud of my accomplishment. I chirped to Michael, "Sweetheart, I've been gardening! Look what I've cut." The most incredulous look spread across my husband's face, his eyes open nearly as wide as his mouth. "Lynni, that isn't gardening! Join me sometime when I weed, hoe, seed, and water. There are gardeners and garden-gatherers. You are *not* a gardener!"

My friend Emilie Barnes says:

I am convinced that gardens are for gardeners and nongardeners alike. A garden is the source of two separate experiences, two different satisfactions. There is gardening, and there is being in a garden.... It is the experience of just being in a garden, enjoying a garden, gratefully gathering the gifts that the garden has to offer—this is the garden experience anyone can have.

I am a garden-gazer. I love just being in gardens, ringed in rainbow hues, gathering gifts of solitude, silence, and scent. I find the garden's sweet serenity mysteriously intoxicating.

And garden-goers like me share this secret: Anyone can be a spiritual gardener. The garden is a heavenly retreat, a haven for spiritual growth

It was the sweetest, most mysterious-looking place anyone could imagine.... And the secret garden bloomed and bloomed and every morning revealed new miracles.

FRANCES HODGSON BURNETT

and renewal. As English poet Dorothy Frances Gurney recognized, "One is nearer God's heart in a garden than anywhere else on earth." In this peaceful paradise—this secret sanctuary created by His own hands—we can walk and talk with our Maker and discover His secrets for living and loving. In the solitude of the garden, we can intimately pray to God, Who loves us—Who is "in the secret place."

I like to think of my journal metaphorically, as the secret garden of my soul, an allusion to the children's book *The Secret Garden*. As a spoiled rich girl and her invalid cousin learn difficult lessons while transforming a dying "secret garden" into a flowering Eden, her personality and his health similarly flourish. The two are restored. Voltaire said, "We must cultivate our garden." As I commune with God in the secret garden—my journal—my heart is cultivated. God waters and feeds my spirit, plants seeds of love and truth, and uproots wildfire weeds of sin that threaten my growth. He restores my soul.

The lovely hymn, "In the Garden," by C. Austin Miles describes a secret garden of restoration, where the grief-stricken Mary Magdalene met Jesus at the tomb before dawn on the day of His resurrection. I can only imagine her unspeakable joy when the Lord—the One she deeply loved, the One who deeply loved her, the One she had supposed dead—approached her in the garden. I can only imagine the intimacy of their conversation. How often I let the lyrics of this hymn shape my secret-garden rendezvous with the Lover of my soul.

I come to the garden alone.

I desire silence and solitude to meet with God. Jesus Himself often prayed to His father in "lonely places." How much more do I, who am easily distracted by the world's stress and strain, need to be alone with God? Gordon MacDonald explains:

Few of us can fully appreciate the terrible conspiracy of noise there is about us, noise that denies us the silence and solitude we need for this cultivation of the inner garden…. There must be times of rhythmic withdrawal. There must be those moments when we break from routines, from other relationships, from the demands of the outer world to meet Him in the garden.

I usually meet God alone in my study, where we won't be interrupted. But my journal is a portable feast. I also enjoy variety and occasionally spice up my dates with God. I write to Him as I sit by myself in a museum, a hotel lobby, a restaurant, or a park, under white-saucered dogwoods. In these rendezvous, I welcome muffled background sounds like clinking cutlery and velveted voices that don't disturb my thoughts.

I adore meeting alone with God in a sidewalk café or tearoom in the late afternoon. Just as the server pours my tea, I pour out my soul to God. Sometimes curious passersby ask what I am writing in "that book." Knowing that the Lord loves this interruption, I smile and say, "I'm writing my love letters to God." They either slowly back away or, I hope, ask about the One with whom I'm corresponding.

While the dew
is still on the roses.

When I was a college vocal major, I sang a gorgeous French art song called "L'Heure Exquise," "The Exquisite Hour." Scripture calls us to pray anytime and all the time, but to me there is something especially exquisite about the morning hour, when dawn's pearly palette illumines the sky. I pray when the day is dew-fresh to gain God's strength for today's difficulties and glean His perspective for tomorrow's questions.

Yet when my daughter, Sheridan, was a baby, she too thought morning enchanting and rose by dawn's early light. Adopting the British custom, I simply moved my feast to four in the afternoon and relished having high tea with Jesus. With Sheridan napping and Michael at work, the Lord and I shared a cup of tea and the confection of communion in my journal.

And the voice I hear falling on my ear
　　the Son of God discloses.
He speaks, and the sound of His voice
　　is so sweet the birds hush their
singing, And the melody that He gave to me
　　within my heart is ringing.

The more time I spend alone with God in my journal-garden, the more I recognize His sweet, sweet voice. Asking God to speak, I listen as I pray, and the Holy Spirit often discloses His message to me as I write.

Gordon MacDonald asserts, "The main value of a journal is as a tool for listening to the quiet Voice that comes out of the garden of the private world. Journal-keeping serves as a wonderful tool for withdrawing and communing with the Father. When I write, it is as if I am in direct conversation with Him."

As I pray in the garden, in my journal, I expect to hear His still, small voice. I listen until the melody He gives me is ringing so deeply in my heart that it hushes the world's noise—that it hushes even birdsong.

And He walks with me, and He talks with me,
　　and He tells me I am His own;
And the joy we share as we tarry there,
　　none other has ever known.

Walking and talking take time, and so does writing. Whenever I tarry, remain, delay, I wait expectantly upon God. Quaker Thomas R. Kelly believed, "We have hints that there is a way of life vastly richer and deeper than all this hurried existence, a life of unhurried serenity and peace and power." Tarrying in my garden paves a path for richness in my relationship with God, depth of insight into His ways, and powerful transformation by His Spirit. Tarrying paves the way for me to experience joy in the Lord.

As I have discovered, "We are considerably poorer if we do not take the time to be with God in the garden, asking Him to interpret the gifts budding, ready to bloom in every event in our lives." Communing in the garden has become so precious to me that I don't begrudge the time; I make room for it. It is the highlight of my day, from which all my life is interpreted—from which all my life's gifts blossom.

And love is the greatest gift: "Love is the fairest bloom in God's garden." When I take time to walk and talk with God in the secret garden of my soul—my journal—the greatest miracle, the deepest secret of life is revealed: "He tells me I am His own." *His own!* God loves me because I am His! I never need doubt that "I am my lover's and my lover is mine." I never need doubt that He will always be. It is a joy known only by those who have spent time alone with God in the garden.

My lover has gone
down to his garden,
to the beds of spices,
to browse in the gardens
and to gather lilies.
I am my lover's and
my lover is mine;
he browses among
the lilies.

SONG OF SONGS 6:2-3

Bye-Bye Blackbird!

*I*T WAS LIKE A SCENE from Hitchcock's *The Birds*.... Perched in profusion in the tangled net of oak branches webbing the wintry sky were crows, more crows, myriad crows—brash, brazen, boisterous—cawing raucously like doomsday prophets, disrupting my peace. I had never seen or *heard* anything like this bird-blitz—except in the movie, and I had presumed that sound to be faked. Yet these birds were real, seeming suddenly to blanket our oaks. The trees were black with them.

How had they come? Suddenly? No... While I was writing my prayers, I had occasionally looked out the window into the backyard and noticed a crow or two peppering the branches; then, from time to time, I saw several more alight. One by one, bird by bird, they had come. Absorbed in my writing, I had forgotten about them until their numbers and noise could not be ignored. They were more than a distraction. They were a disquieting presence that had ruined my serenity and sojourn with God.

As ridiculous as it may seem, I opened the window and shouted at them to leave, but to no avail. The pesky crows maintained their post. Then Pete, our gallant neighbor, charged out his back door and, armed with a BB gun, shot decisively overhead. *Pop. Pop. Pop.* In a blink the crows were gone, a thunder of wings beating the air.

For some odd reason, maybe because of the crows' ebony color, I recalled the song Grandma Nina used to sing when I was small: "Pack up all my care and woe, here I go singing low, Bye-Bye Blackbird." The crows were now blackbirds symbolizing cares, woes, and

Blackbird, Blackbird, singing the blues all day
Right outside of my door
Blackbird, Blackbird, why do you sit and say,
"There's no sunshine in store"?
All through the winter you hung around
Now I begin to feel homeward bound.
Blackbird, Blackbird, gotta be on my way
Where there's sunshine galore.

MORT DIXON

worries—worries that had multiplied in my life, one by one, bird by bird.

Worries...how I hated them. I was the world's worst worry-wart. My active imagination could magnify showers into tempests, molehills into mountain ranges, sniffles into terminal illnesses. Yet I knew this was wrong. Jesus tells us repeatedly not to worry. The apostle Paul insists that we should be anxious for nothing. I knew I was making myself sick—sick of mind.

As the sun set and darkness engulfed me, a deeper darkness descended—a winter of worries, of blackbirds burgeoning in my mind. I began sketching a stick-figure tree with numerous lines jutting helter-skelter like my thoughts. One by one, bird by bird, I listed my cares on the crisscrossed branches. The birds—some large, some small—that had been caged in my mind and caroming crazily around, now flew freely and landed as fast as I could write: *Gotta cut down on fat. Watching too much TV. Clear the clutter! Sheridan rejecting me. Why'd I leave career??*

What a lousy mother! Wish I'd taken dream job. Sick of living in "wilderness." Need adult company. Mike's over fifty—will die of heart attack! What if Sheridan kidnapped? Can't live without her, Mike, parents. Will never write book. Clothes outdated—no $ for new ones. More kitchen floor tiles loosening—ugh!—no $ for repairs. Organize files and recipes. Photos getting ruined—remove from plastic albums! Print business cards. Read entire Bible this year. Afraid of getting breast cancer! Write parenting article. Afraid to meet new people. Past sin still haunts me.... The list flew frantically on.

When I'd finally finished having my own bird-blitz—after I'd allowed those carping crows to have their say in writing—the once-pristine journal page was covered, but my head was clear. I drew a deep breath, felt amazing relief, *and* made a connection. When I had lifted my pen, I was like Pete shooting his BB gun. When I took aim in my journal, I was saying, "Bye-bye, blackbirds!" and the worries began to flee.

With them out of my head and onto the page, they had lost their power. Seeing my concerns in black and white—concerns both real and imagined—allowed me detachment and objectivity.

In my journal, I began studying the patterns of my birds, lifting them with my pen from the branches of my "worry tree" and caging them in orderly lists: These birds could be delegated; these could be forgotten; these could be confessed; these could be acted upon; these could be lifted up to God for His intervention; these could be entrusted to His care; these could be considered masked opportunities if I'd dare to take a risk! The act of writing had brought clarity: "All at once my life [took] sudden shape." Immediately, I wrote to God, confessing, petitioning, praising, and tying everything up with the golden thread of thanksgiving, just as Paul admonishes in Philippians 4:6. And as Paul knew I would, I experienced the peace that transcends understanding.

Martin Luther noted, "We cannot keep the birds from flying over our heads, but we can keep them from nesting in our hair." One way to keep the birds of burden from landing and roosting in our hair, in our minds, is to steer them off-course one by one as they attack, and pen them in our journals through prayer. Once they're captured there, we can move from the winter of oppression into the freedom of His "Son-shine galore." Since that day when I bade the blackbirds bye-bye, I knew I was on the road to freedom. I knew I was "homeward bound."

Who of you by worrying can add
a single hour to his life?

MATTHEW 6:27

Lists of Lament

FROM THE SHOWER STALL, I stared motionlessly through an impressionistic veil of mingling tears and silvery spray at my beautiful Bogey—his limp, black body vanishing behind clouds of steam as rapidly as his life itself was evaporating. In a few short hours, the veterinarian would quietly end Bo's thirteen years of loving and loyal companionship. How ironic to stand over a drain, life draining from me—swirling away in nauseous waves—as I felt Bogey's nearing loss.

> *Little deaths.*
> *Somewhere in*
> *the psyche*
> *all these changes*
> *and losses*
> *register as death.*
>
> JANE KENYON

Gazing through the lens of water-warped glass, I saw a series of Bogey photos emerge like dreamily developing prints—first translucent, then grainy, then dawning clearer and clearer in the darkroom of my memory. As I discovered images I had captured in the past, I could almost hear the sound of a camera shutter triggering each remembrance.

Click: Bogey is a puppy, a tiny poodle-puddle of soft, curly fur spreading across my lap as Michael drives us home from the breeder, swearing he will *never* walk such an effeminate dog! "We're naming him Bubba!" he threatens, brandishing the bully-name like a club.

Click: Bogey needs no lessons in bravado. At every ring of the doorbell, his booming voice bellows from his deceptively small form. He *is* tough—a warrior watchdog!

Click: Attila the poodle-puppy goes on a killing spree, teething everything in his sight. Even my new Bible has bitten the dust.

Click: Bogey is mature, the fur on his legs ballooning like Aladdin's pantaloons. There will be no typical topiary cut for this suave Standard.

Click: I hear toe-tapping on the hallway floor. Looking up, I see that my buddy has come to keep me company as I wrestle-write. I detest that words won't come and tell him so. He cocks his head knowingly, then gives me an "All better!" kiss.

Click: I am vocalizing at our piano, practicing for an audition. As usual, I have competition. Bogey, head flung back with abandon, is howling like a banshee—a regular poodle Pavarotti, whose top notes, embarrassingly, are higher than mine.

Click: Now my canine countertenor is virtually silent, save his shallow breathing, which becomes increasingly sporadic and labored...and soon will cease.

The clock's chime interrupted my retro-reverie. Sheridan, unaware of the day's looming horror, would be home from school soon. I stepped from the shower, toweling water droplets and tears, determined to be strong for her.

When Michael brought Sheridan home, we tried desperately to explain the inexplicable. Adult logic, "God's timing," and the vet's best "You don't want him to suffer" advice offered little comfort to a ten-year-old about to lose her lifelong love. Wrung from somewhere down deep in her gut came a raw, haunting, unearthly wail that shattered our hearts. We were helpless. With great reluctance and wavering resolve, we gently laid our rag-doll dog in the jeep-turned-hearse and made that last lonely drive. I *resolved* not to cry.

On the way to the vet's, I retrieved a faded photo-memory of another joyless journey, this one from my childhood. Click: I am eleven and am bookended between relatives in the backseat of a black limousine. We lead the slow, sad procession to Oak Grove Cemetery, where we will gently lay to rest *my* lifelong love, Grandpa. Aunt Alice admonishes, "Stop crying, honey. You have to be brave for your grandmother." Trying to hold in every last tear, I squeeze my eyes so hard they hurt.

In the days after Bogey's death, whenever I mentioned missing my cuddly companion, my only company all day, every day, I received new admonitions to buck up from other wise ones in my life. "What's the big deal? He's just a dog...." "Come on, Lynn, Sheridan's the one who should be sad...." "Get over it. Get a grip. Get a puppy...." And with well-meaning if misguided compassion, Michael removed from our home every last trace of Bogey—his bowls and bones, his balls and blankets. These remainders were but painful reminders, surely best taken from my sight. The unspoken message was loud and clear: Don't talk, don't cry, don't remember. Yet somewhere subconsciously in my psyche, the pain registered.

Autumn followed summer. Activity followed sedentary days. Work filled both my hours and the grave-deep hole in my heart. Life crowded out memories of

Bogey's death and then of his life. Had I only imagined him? Soon, it seemed, his very memory would be buried.

But ironically, on November 11, Veterans Day, a long-buried memory was exhumed as I watched television. A documentary highlighted the Vietnam Veterans Memorial—that boundless black wall etched with numberless names—names of thousands and thousands of young Americans, names written in bravery and in blood.

Click: I am fifteen, chatting and flirting with Ralphie in his driveway after a rehearsal for *South Pacific*. We were high school and church chums who could talk about everything or nothing—those sometimes serious, often silly teenage talks. But this talk turned dead-serious. Unexpectedly, our pastor arrived. Reverend Steinmeier didn't exit his car alone. A somber soldier accompanied him and urged Ralphie to get his parents. All I remember is that, when Mrs. Nixon saw the officer, she collapsed, sobbing, into her husband's arms. She *knew*. A mother knew that her beloved son

Donald was gone. The war had come home and killed her heart. Ralphie and I suddenly embraced; we were really embracing the pain.

As my thoughts drifted back to the present, I resumed watching television as mourners searched endless lists for just one name—for just one memory, for just one proof that their beloved had lived and died and was honored and remembered. When they found that name, they lingered, fingering it gently, reverently. The memorial is sometimes called the "healing wall." Its architect, Maya Ying Lin, understood that we must *name* our grief. Those who died were not a number on a military dog tag; each one had a name—first name, middle name, nickname, surname. Each person had blossomed from a family, a history, a life-and-breath reality; each one had loved and been loved, had laughed and lamented. Lin realized that when we name our grief, we acknowledge it, embrace it, lance it before the unnamed pain grows, festers, and consumes us. Naming our grief is the first step toward healing.

The morning after I watched the television documentary, during my quiet time with God, I read my "daily" psalm and was surprised by David's words: "Record my lament; list my tears on Your scroll—are they not in Your record?" I didn't remember ever reading that David asked God to record his tears. Just as with the war memorial, David was naming his grief and asking God to keep track with a list.

I don't fully know what compelled me—perhaps reading this verse, perhaps thinking about death and Vietnam the day before—but somehow I knew I must go to the cemetery that afternoon. Yet I fought the idea. I hated Oak Grove and only went when expected at a family graveside service. There had, however, been a recent exception. In September, at our Uncle Lawrence's request, Michael and I had placed pink carnations on Aunt Francie's grave to commemorate her birthday. Though both she and her sister, Aunt Mart, had died a couple years before, I was overcome by the wave of grief that suddenly engulfed me. *Where on earth is this coming from? God, why am I feeling this way? I should be over this! And we have an appointment. I can't cry! Mike and I have to go!* I was that eleven-year-old child again, mustering every ounce of strength to squeeze back my tears.

With the pain from that experience still fresh, I didn't want to go to the cemetery again. A debate began in my mind: *I have a writing deadline; I don't have time for this.... But I have to go now; this may be the last mild day in months.... Go to a cemetery alone? What will I do there? This is bizarre!* God's words cut through the chaos: *I want you to go and settle unfinished business.* I recognized the Lord's nudging and prepared to leave. As an afterthought, I grabbed my journal and headed out the door.

The day was warm and welcoming; the cemetery, serene. Honeyed sunlight streamed through bare branches like rib-boned gold. Brown-sugar leaves streuseled the moist earth and covered our family's flat gravestones. One by one, stone after stone, I brushed the leaves away to expose eighteen graves.

Dear God! Eighteen! Oh, God, so many! I realized and shuddered. Slowly, I read all eighteen names—names of loved ones I'd admired, names of those I'd adored. Reading each name renewed my pain and revealed my profound loss.

Then I saw Grandpa's stone. *Grandpa! Grandpa!* I sank to my knees—and sank to the end of my defenses. Deep inside I felt a wrenching, a wresting, as something terribly tenacious struggled to break free. It was that "inner silent wail that cannot be muffled." I remembered Sheridan's wail and knew that I,

too, had wailed, but in silence, in suffering. I was silent no more. Grief finally broke from my soul, loosing sob after heartrending sob.

Those tears were but prelude to more. Again I recognized that still, small voice: *Record your lament. List your tears.* I wasn't comprehending. *What do You mean? What more do You want, God?* I struggled, wiping my eyes. *Get your journal.* My journal. Now I understood. Shaken, I walked to the car, got my journal, and sat against the solid trunk of a leafless oak.

Dipping my pen into my heart's inkwell of tears, I streamed lists of laments into my journal. I finally let myself feel the pain that had so long been silent. I named my griefs, those scores of sorrows that had unknowingly multiplied and festered. Piercing each wound with my pen, I listed tears for those I'd lost: my grandparents, aunts, and uncles; my cousin, Holly, who died of heart failure at twenty-five; an exquisitely beautiful high-school friend later murdered by her husband; a church acquaintance whom I'd barely noticed, not knowing that his loneliness would lead to suicide; the reclusive neighbor we'd befriended who died of a massive stroke *before* receiving my overdue thank-you letter; and my octogenarian mentor, Myrtle, with whom I wished I'd spent more time.

I listed tears for those I couldn't bear the thought of losing: my beloved mother and father; precious older friends; and our dear friend, Frank, who was dying of cancer and recently had asked me to sing at his funeral. I listed tears for the dying and the suffering, for babies aborted in wombs and youth aborted in wars, and for other kinds of losses I'd experienced: betrayal by a trusted friend and irreconcilable differences with another; divorces of friends who'd had fairy-tale marriages; the razing of our "happily-ever-after" bungalow that housed twenty-four years of memories and the felling of the grand old oak that had shaded us there; the loss of my youth, innocence, and wasted years of depression; Michael's near-fatal heart attack and his precarious future; the ending of Sheridan's childhood; and the death of some dreams: relinquishing a professional singing career, refusing a long-desired job in order to raise Sheridan, never living in a Victorian house. They were all losses and changes, great and small. They were large and little deaths that I had never mourned, for which I had never sought God's comfort.

Shakespeare said, "Give sorrow words. The grief that does not speak whispers the o'erfraught heart and bids it break." Grief had been whispering its message to me for years, but I had refused to receive it. My heart had been silently breaking. But as I "spoke sorrow" in prayer in my journal, something astonishing occurred: I was gradually being transformed. My heartbreak quietly, slowly, at first imperceptibly, began breaking into joy. *Joy?* I was incredulous. I began to understand Elizabeth Barrett Browning's insight that "grief may be joy misunderstood."

As I listed my laments, I experienced piercing pain yet, simultaneously, the mysterious release of it. As I wrote, I realized I wasn't just enduring the pain, but reliving the pleasure, the overwhelming pleasure of having loved and been loved by extraordinary people: "My tears declared an unspoken, grieving thank you for [their] having been a part of my life." These dear ones had bequeathed to me love, laughter, faith, fearlessness, comfort, compassion, wisdom, and wonder. Inexplicably, remembrance's requiem intensified my appreciation for those I love now. This became a wake-up call to honor my family and friends with time and tenderness, never again to take them for granted. Unexpectedly, I, too, could give thanks for the death of dreams; their end had marked the beginning of better ones.

Although still feeling the pain of life's losses, I was no longer despondent. Instead I was deepened by what I'd gained—those intangible treasures I had inherited that could never be stolen by death. Gratitude to God welled up in me like a fountain overflowing in praise. As poet Edwin Markham understood, "Only the soul that knows the mighty grief can know the mighty rapture. Sorrow comes to stretch out spaces in the heart for joy." I was ready to receive them both.

Weeping may remain for a night,
but rejoicing comes in the morning.

PSALM 30:5

I Only Have Eyes for You

*I*T WAS CHRISTMASTIME. We had just moved into a sprawling ranch house after living twenty-four years in a charming little bungalow. I felt as if I'd left my heart and a lifetime of precious memories behind. *Oh, God, how can I experience Christmas joy in this "foreign" place?* I wondered....

As I often do when depressed, I asked God to comfort me through the psalms. That day I happened to turn to Psalm 81: "You shall have no foreign god among you; you shall not bow down to an alien god. I am the LORD your God.... Open wide your mouth and I will fill it" (vv. 9-10). I saw little inspiration in these strange-sounding words, even though the psalm promised ultimate satisfaction. *Great, Lord! I thought. I want joy, and You talk about*

> Turn your eyes
> upon Jesus;
> Look full in His
> wonderful face,
> And the things of
> earth will grow
> strangely dim
> In the light of
> His glory and grace.
>
> HELEN H. LEMMEL

idols and wide mouths! I don't understand what You're saying, but I open my heart and ask You to fill me with Your presence.

I decided to go shopping, thinking that if I bought some special Christmas decorations for the new house to make it really *mine*, I'd experience a little joy.

I had my heart set on hand-blown golden ornaments, but was unprepared for the price. *Ouch!* Our ordinary old ornaments would have to do. *Surely we can update my pitiful childhood Nativity set,* I consoled myself. I spied a gorgeous set made of cream-colored china elegantly accented with gold. The baby Jesus was especially exquisite— and so was the price! I grew more discouraged by the minute.

Forgetting decorations altogether, I went to the jewelry department. I had always wanted a sapphire ring. Though I knew I couldn't afford one, I thought just looking would be fun. Yet window-shopping only fueled my discontent.

With my shop-for-joy trip a dismal failure, I headed for the exit as tinny mall Muzak whined Santa songs. Racing out the door, I almost ran over a little high-school choir caroling in the frosty air. There was poignancy in their presence, simplicity in their song. I, and a young mother holding a beautiful baby boy, were the only shoppers who had stopped to hear a young teen's plaintive solo: "Sweet little Jesus boy... We didn't know who You was." His velvety voice floated on the air like softly falling snow. The baby cooed. I listened to the entire song. Then, with moist eyes, I hugged the singer, grateful for his gift of joy, the first I'd experienced all day.

Approaching my car, I stopped to gaze at a distant row of pear trees, their bright gold leaves flashing like bangles in the jewel-blue sky. I could hear the sharp intake of my own breath, surprised as I was by this sudden beauty.

A quick glance at my watch cut short my enjoyment; I needed to reach the hardware store before it closed. Completely exasperated when the salesman told me that he'd sold the last set of icicle lights (the kind I had wanted to buy for *several* years), I drove home in the dark in a foul mood, without Christmas lights, without Christmas joy.

I parked the car and stepped out. Glancing upward, I was mesmerized by thousands of glittering stars—like crystal confetti scattered across the moonlit sky. *It doesn't matter if we don't have lights,* I realized. *Lord, we have Your glorious galaxies!*

The truth dawned forcefully. Because I had opened my heart to God's presence, He removed my fake idols and filled my day with His *real* treasures. Instead of golden ornaments and a sapphire ring, He gave me gold leaves and a turquoise sky; instead of commercial Muzak, the genuine Christmas message in a stirring spiritual; instead of a lifeless china Jesus, a precious living baby—a reminder of the vulnerable child Jesus born just for me; and instead of a string of light bulbs that would soon dim, a starry host that would blaze eternally.

When would I ever learn? How often would I settle for life's tinsel instead of God's treasure, for cheap imitations and unsatisfying substi-tutes instead of His genuine gifts of glory? How often would I suc-cumb to the worldly lure of "lesser gods" when I could experience *real life* and all the blessings offered by the one and only God?

I was a shamefully slow student. One glance through my journals was like taking inventory of the shelves of a golden-calf curio shop. I found molds for my own idol-making as well as diminutive deities that had threatened my love and loyalty to God because they had captured my time, attention, and heart. These repeated struggles, preserved in writing, proved how often I had failed to trash my trinkets. Like A. W. Tozer, I had admitted more than once, "Father, I want to know Thee, but my cowardly heart fears to give up its toys. I cannot part with them without inward bleeding, and I do not try to hide from Thee the terror of the parting." Some "toys" seemed harmless, others horren-dous, but all of them had, from time to time, insidiously replaced God on His throne in my heart.

Among my toys were those mysteriously multiplying teddy bears. I'm not quite sure how it happened…. I bought two tiny teddies, and they proliferated when I wasn't looking, running absolutely amuck. When there was no longer room for Michael to sleep in our bed, he issued an ultimatum: "Either the bears go or I will!" I contemplated buying another bed for the bears, but instead the bears went. When I ended that collection, I just started new ones. I accumulated rocks, thimbles, teacups, china, dolls, prints, postcards, videos, jewelry, clothes, shoes, magazines, and hundreds of books. Anne Morrow Lindbergh consid-ered that, "The collector walks with blinders on; he sees nothing but the prize." In stockpiling these prizes, I was spiritually blind, missing *the* Prize, the only One worth possessing—the only One who could satisfy.

Other icons that had blinded my eternal view were my addictions to alcohol and food; television news, "soaps," and sitcoms; e-mail; professional memberships; volunteer activities; church work, overwork, and pious perfectionism. I was even addicted to my own singing, speaking, and writing, loving nothing more than listening to my own tapes or reading my own words! As clergyman Richard Baxter realized, "We are naturally our own idols." If I had ever doubted it (and I had), I needed only to look honestly in my journals to be exposed to the glaring golden-calf glow of my admitted compulsions. My writing permitted no lies.

Yet, thankfully, my journals were also like an apothecary's mortar, gritty with traces of fool's gold from gods I had ground with my pestle-pen. Through confession and repentance, I finally relinquished them to the one true God. Seeing those same idols appear repeatedly in my writing had forced me to see that I had not done business with God.

And, mercifully, God had not done business with me. In Old Testament times, His punishment for idolatry was severe. When Aaron and the Israelites reeled in revelry, dancing their golden-calf conga at the foot of Mount Sinai, God's anger burned. Their destruction was sure. But Moses pleaded for the people, and God stayed His hand.

Yet Jesus, my advocate, *opens* His hands—hands that were nailed to a cross for my idolatry. Because of Jesus' payment for my sins, God forgives my idol worship and gives me the power, in turn, to crucify it. Author Leslie Williams maintains:

Because of the cross, we are freed from the trappings of idolatry. As Christians seeking Jesus, our eyes are opened more and more as we grope toward the light of God's truth.... If we let Him, like a loving parent Jesus gently takes our faces, cupping His hand under our chins, and turns our sight away from the world's attractive lures, then refocuses our vision on Him.

As one wise believer knew, "Looking unto Jesus. Only three little words, but in those three little words is the whole secret of life." As I look to Jesus raised on the cross, as I look to Jesus revealed in God's Word, as I look to Jesus reflected in my journal, where I have committed to meet with Him daily, He enables me to look away from the world. My journals are dark glass, but the more I commune with Him there, the more I am changed—the more I can see His image faintly shining in the pages. When I only have eyes for Jesus, I need nothing more. I am satisfied. My golden calves grow strangely dim in the light of His glory and grace.

Then the Lord said to Moses, "...your people, whom you brought up out of Egypt, have become corrupt. They have been quick to turn away from what I have commanded them and have made themselves an idol cast in the shape of a calf. They have bowed down to it."

EXODUS 32:7-8

Letting Go

The fruit
of letting go
is birth.

MEISTER ECKHART

I HAD BEEN MARRIED for seventeen years when, for my fortieth birthday, God delivered a surprise package wrapped in pink: a precious baby daughter named Sheridan. She is a treasure I absolutely cherish, but one I initially struggled to receive.

I had never wanted to be a mother; the prospect frightened me to death. I was intimidated by the enormous responsibility of raising a child as well as by my many personal inadequacies. I knew nothing about children, and I had a difficult time interacting with them. I had a morbid fear of dying in childbirth, which having a child at forty only exacerbated. I was petrified! Numerous things could go wrong with the baby or with me.

Even if the pregnancy were uncomplicated, I dreaded the long haul, feeling as if I would be raising a child until I was eighty! How would I survive? Where would I find the physical stamina necessary to keep pace with an active toddler? How could I have the fortitude to combat the twenty-first-century evils that would undermine my parenting at every turn? The big picture overwhelmed me, and I felt trapped.

A well-meaning Christian friend suggested abortion. Her advice only increased my struggle. I knew that this child was not a cosmic accident, but was God's creation, whom He was intricately knitting together in my womb. I didn't doubt God's will, yet I fought intensely against accepting it. I felt extremely pressured by my own deepening fear of so many unknowns.

In a Bible study I was doing at the time, the brave words of the Virgin Mary, whose circumstances were far more difficult than mine, shone like a beacon, illuminating my darkness, granting me courage, and giving me hope. I read Luke's account of the Annunciation when the angel Gabriel descended with the grandeur of great wings and with glorious yet grave news: Mary would be overshadowed by the power of the Holy Spirit—her will overshadowed by His—in order for her to conceive the inconceivable. She, a mere mortal, would birth the awesome Son of God.

Elisabeth Elliot expounds, "[Mary] did not give way to fear. She said, 'Behold...the handmaid of the Lord,' putting herself instantly at His disposal, an act of unreserved self-donation and perfect surrender. She was attentive, willing, and ready to receive the Lord's word." But was I ready? Would I "wholeheartedly surrender to God, leaving quietly with Him all the 'what ifs' and 'but what abouts'"? Would I "truthfully say to Him, 'Anything You choose for me, Lord—to have, to be, to do, or to suffer? I am at Your orders? I have no agenda of my own'"?

My journal became a battleground for the war of the wills—mine against God's. There I could agonize freely about my struggle and frailty. There I could finally acquiesce to my God. I penned this prayer of ultimate acceptance:

Dear Lord, my body contains a secret seed, immortally conceived, mortally sown. Momentarily, I enfold creation. A fragment of eternity forms concentrically like a pearl. Oh God! Can I bear the weight of priceless cargo? Can my broken vessel store treasure of such worth? Can my earthen jar contain a soul outlasting every star? Can I refuse? Can I uproot the hidden seed? Can I coerce my Potter to remold the brittle clay—remake my fragile vessel for some other use?

I can consent. I can surrender to

Your engendering Spirit. I can open myself freely to Your infilling glory. I am willing to unveil the pearl at any price. I will become a chalice for my Maker's grace. Behold, Your servant. Let it be to me as You have said.

Although I refused to abort, I didn't gracefully surrender to motherhood as Mary did. I rebelliously complained, questioning God's wisdom and resenting His timing: *How could this child be a gift? How could I raise her when I didn't even know how to change a diaper? How could I leave a twenty-year career and financial security? Wouldn't I look ridiculous as a forty-year-old dinosaur swapping diaper-rash remedies with my twenty-year-old counterparts?*

Although my emotions vacillated between anger and apathy, I prayed that God would change my heart, grant me courage, and endow me with motherly feelings. I clung to the truth that, despite my opinion, this child was God's gift and blessing.

Then it happened. From the moment I first held Sheridan, God miraculously replaced my callous heart of stone with a mother's heart of tenderness. I wrote in my journal: "Oh, God! Now that I see, touch, and talk to her, everything—absolutely everything—is different! Oh, God, thank You. Thank You. Thank You for my beautiful baby!"

God had changed my heart, and now He would change my world. The more I was with Sheridan, the more I adored her and began desiring to be with her all the time. Yet, paradoxically, the more I began to sense God guiding me to end my career, the more I battled against Him. Daily I fumed frustration onto journal pages that became "wrestling mats in miniature" for my Lord and me.

Poet Luci Shaw reasons, "Writing will help us sort out the contradictions we see within ourselves...and to work through them and begin to find a foundational integrity before God. When we are wrestling with God, as Jacob did, we are at least in close contact with Him."

The closer I drew to God in the passionate, wrestling embrace of prayer, the more honest I became. As I wrote, God helped me sort out my contradictions—that no matter how much I loved Sheridan and felt great responsibility in my new identity as her mother, I was actually fearing that I would lose the only identity I had ever known. I feared sinking into deep depression in the isolation of my home. In the past, God had used employment to help me overcome seasons of despair by involving me with people and meaningful work, giving my life purpose. I clung desperately to comfortable surroundings, a respectable income, professional friends, and personal recognition. I could not comprehend A. W. Tozer's claim that "in the kingdom of God the surest way to lose something is to try to protect it, and the best way to keep it is to let it go." The fruit of letting go is birth and new life.

But the Lord was about to teach me this lesson by patiently prying loose my grip. One weekend as I walked in autumn woods, God guided me with the image of gently falling leaves. I watched as colorful leaves clung tenaciously to branches, struggling to hold on. Then, as if by some knowledge of God's command, with each gust of wind, they simply let go. When they did, they began a graceful waltz, pirouetting with abandon in the breeze. Beauty and freedom characterized their release. At that moment, God whispered, "Lynn, let go!" I gave my employer notice, committing myself to whatever dance God was choreographing.

Soon it was wintertime outside, and it felt like winter within me—a time of depression, doubt, and loneliness. I was a winter tree, stripped of the lush leafage of professional purpose, accolades, and friendships. Yet I knew that though the tree looked dead, it lived; its life wasn't in its leaves, but in its roots. I knew that as I rooted myself in God, I'd bear fruit in the future.

I also knew that trees don't sin by complaining. They bloom in season; and in times of barrenness, their leafless limbs raise in praise to their Maker. Freed of foliage, they have an unparalleled opportunity to hold stars, shining like jewels, in their branches. In my stripped condition, I decided to grasp the stars of life I'd been too blind to see. Every day I recorded my blessings in my journal, discovering a host of unexpected luminaries lighting my darkness like sparkling constellations of joy.

When God brought me home to raise Sheridan, He unexpectedly fulfilled my dream of becoming an author, a dream that full-time work didn't permit. He also unexpectedly transformed me through the influence of my little girl. She was my "midlife replacement therapy"—replacing my lethargy with her energy, my depression with her joy, my cynicism with her optimism, my jadedness with her innocence, my workaholism with her play. I grew mentally as she and I explored her world, emotionally as Michael and I drew closer to each other in raising her, and spiritually as I became completely dependent upon God for my mothering.

Luci Shaw concludes, "If I am willing to abandon myself to God, He will give me back myself, my identity." God had given me back my *true* self. Now I knew that my identity was in Christ alone and not in my profession.

When, like Mary, I said, "Let it be"—when, like the autumn leaf, I let go—I entered the beauty of God's dance, finally free to follow Him only, knowing that the only place into which I could fall was the palm of my Partner's hand.

Then Mary said, "Behold the maidservant of the Lord! Let it be to me according to your word."

LUKE 1:38, NKJV

Oceans of Mercy, Oceans of Love

WOMEN, CURLED LIKE FETUSES,
lay in deep recliners, cocooned in blankets
that muffled their cries but couldn't hide
their trembling. In the garish glare of flickering fluorescents, I saw their tear-stained faces
and terrified eyes. *Maybe it's because most of
them are teenagers*, I reasoned silently, per-
plexed by their dramatic reactions. I didn't cry
at all....

Over twenty-five years later, I still wonder what happened to those nameless, tor-
tured souls, now older, now absorbed
anonymously into society. People know
them, but not their secret. They belong to
the Post-Abortion Society, and they
carefully guard their identities
and their atrocities.

O the deep,
deep love of Jesus,
vast, unmeasured,
boundless, free!
Rolling as a mighty ocean
in its fullness over me!

SAMUEL TREVOR FRANCIS

I know. I'm one of them.

Ironically, when I became a lifetime member, I was unaware of the club I had joined or the exorbitant membership dues I would pay. At the time, I was oblivious to any abortion aftermath. I felt free.

Following my abortion that blazing-blue summer afternoon, I went to my favorite restaurant, where I read a book to occupy my mind with anything but "the procedure." I felt nothing—no guilt, no sadness, no regret. I felt only relief—relief from the relentless nausea and the gripping fear that had threatened my future.

The months that followed were a frenzied blur of painting classes, voice lessons, career-climbing, and soul-searching with friends at a sidewalk bar-café. Tête-à-tête, glass-to-glass, we sipped our wine and shared our dreams long into those neon nights. Slowly, insidiously, my life acquired a seedy side, predominated by a love for alcohol. I couldn't stop drinking.

Then God graciously intervened. Unexpectedly, Gary Buchanan, an old high-school friend, visited me at work to share his excitement in receiving Jesus

Christ as his Savior and Lord. I was astounded. Gary was completely trans-formed, miraculously freed from past addictions and gloriously on fire for Jesus. Comparing my life with his, I was deeply ashamed. Gary lovingly but firmly urged me to turn to God.

Desperate for God, I began seeking Him each morning with journal and Bible in hand. I penned letters of love and longing—longing for healing and restoration. God met me in my prayers and transformed me through His Word, showing me the truth—that drinking wine was "dissipation." He gave me the courage and power to stop.

He also showed me another truth that I, still a new Christian, didn't recall ever seeing. I read Psalm 139 with new eyes and deepening horror: "For you created my inmost being; you knit me together in my mother's womb. I praise you because I am fearfully and wonderfully made.... My frame was not hidden from you when I was made in the secret place....Your eyes saw my unformed body. All the days ordained for me were written in your book before one of them came to be" (vv. 13-16).

These words of profound wonder and beauty were, for me, like pierc-ing daggers, stabbing my heart, mind, and soul. Astounded, I wrote in my Bible, "God, You planned us intricately. You meant for all babies to be born!" *All!* For the first time I truly understood that I had taken a child's life. Overcome with guilt, I confessed my heinous sin in my jour-nal, experiencing the pain of betraying God. Yet I felt no personal loss. I was emotionally dead.

In the ensuing years, God gradually began to confront me with my past by exposing me to pro-life literature and post-abortive testimonies. As I listened to grief-stricken women, I realized that following my abortion I had dulled my conscience with alcohol and activities, hiding my heart under a protective armor that was now slowly being penetrated. Many years after the abortion, I finally started to feel personal pain and genuine sympathy toward the tiny child I had destroyed. I imagined her to be a girl, and she was real to me.

In the midst of this emotional upheaval, at age forty I became pregnant. I panicked, almost paranoid about pregnancy, the birth process, and the challenges of motherhood. A Christian friend suggested abortion, but this time I was fully aware of the evil I would commit if I took my child's life—if I killed the person God was creating. I couldn't do it. I immediately told family and friends about the pregnancy. There was no turning back.

When Sheridan was born, love completely overwhelmed me. She dazzled me! I adored my baby, my precious gift from God. Yet Sheridan's life underscored the tragic death of my first child, whose cry echoed in my mind like a haunting tune that had no end. She clung tenaciously to me like a fragile apparition that wouldn't let go. Engulfed by guilt, I craved God's peace but couldn't find it. Although God's Word assured me of His forgiveness, I couldn't feel it.

I discovered a post-abortive Bible study group at a pregnancy resource center, where I met women who understood my torment. As their tear-streaked faces contorted in grief over their aborted children, I saw again those frightened faces from long ago. I felt their pain, but still I couldn't cry.

One evening, as we sat in a circle sharing, a water bug brushed my foot, startling me. I was about to stomp on it, but suddenly I froze. I couldn't breathe. I couldn't move. I couldn't kill it. I absolutely could not bring myself to destroy it. *Oh, God!* I screamed silently. *Oh, God! Oh, God! I can't even kill an insect, but I killed...I killed my own baby! Oh, God, I didn't know. I didn't know what I was doing! God, help me. Please, please help me!*

Agony seared my soul. In strobelike flashes, scenes from the abortion jolted my mind—pictures so graphic, so horrific, I could tolerate them only in brief, painful pulses. My armor cracked, then crumbled to my feet. My denial was over. My shield was gone. My wound was raw. My pain was excruciating. I sobbed convulsively, uncontrollably. Finally, I began to grieve openly the death of the little one I had lost—the little one I had come to love, the little one who would never be, the little one I had named Shannon. How could God ever forgive me for murdering my own baby—a baby with a name, a life, a soul? How could I ever forgive myself?

Many more years would pass before I learned those answers. The abortion was my unpardonable sin—until I received God's miraculous healing on a sunny Sunday at the edge of the ocean.

It was the last day of a journaling retreat, and I was the only believer there. Just the day before, in a conversation at lunch, I had explained to the women at my table why abortion was never right—why abortion always took the life of an innocent child. We didn't argue, but they held fast to their viewpoint: Although they would never have one, they said that abortion was a woman's "right to choose." I didn't share my story, but the next afternoon God gave me another opportunity.

As we gathered on sandy sugar-white shores for our last writing assignment, the facilitator asked us to share about a self-inflicted wound from which we had never healed. Then she asked, "What does grace feel like? Do you extend it to yourself or withhold it? Are you ready to forgive yourself?" She recited a little verse: "I want to go where the waters overflow. I'm ready to let them wash over me. If it's love flowing freely, I'm ready. If the waters can redeem me, I'm ready.

I'm ready. I'm ready." The words undulated through my mind like the mighty ocean stretching before me.

The other participants finished their writing and went farther up the beach to share. I stayed behind, mesmerized by the ocean's incessant waves. Their rhythmic pounding scrolled the shore while new hope rolled through my mind: *You're ready. You're ready. You're ready.* I knew it was the Spirit of God. I sensed His divine enabling.

Was I finally ready to receive God's grace? Oh, how I wanted to! Was I finally ready to forgive myself? I knew I had to. C. S. Lewis said, "If God forgives us, we must forgive ourselves. Otherwise it is almost like setting up ourselves as a higher tribunal than He." I, higher than God? Never! This was my moment of reckoning. Jesus had paid for all my sins or none. His atoning blood had cleansed everything or nothing.

As I looked at the endless watery expanse spreading across the horizon of infinity, for the first time in my life I truly sensed the deep, deep love of Jesus. I lifted my pen, and my soul spilled into my journal:

Oh, God! Your grace is fluid, flowing, flooding, unleashed, unlimited, unmeasured, undeserved—a gift bestowed without merit, without cost to me, free—a ceilingless sky, a relentless riot of rain, a shoreless, bottomless ocean, there for the taking by the teaspoonful, cupful, bucketful, basinful, whatever amount for whatever need. And, with the taking, no diminishing supply—unending, unfathomable.

For almost twenty years since the abortion, I've sandbagged the flow of Your grace and lay dying in the sand—parched and shriveled like snakeskin, thick-tongued, cotton-eyed, unable to see or speak or receive forgiveness, unable to walk to the water to plunge my festering heart into Your ocean's depths for cleansing release. I'm Bethesda Pool's paralytic—immobile—waiting for You to stir the waters, lift me up, and put me in to baptize my wounds in the sea of Your grace, to bury my sin in the depths of the ocean. With Your help, I would be satisfied now to swallow even the tiniest raindrop of grace. I'm dying of thirst—thirst for Your love, thirst for Your pardon.

Oh, Lord, I'm ready. I come to the water. Your love flows freely. I'm ready to receive it. Your living waters can redeem me. I'm ready— ready to let Your oceans of mercy, oceans of love, wash over me. I receive now the fullness of the forgiveness You gave when You opened wide your arms on Calvary's cross—when You died for my sin of abortion. Lord, I'm ready. I'm ready.

Torrents of words and tears deluged my journal. For the first time ever, I prayed freely about my emotional pain from the abortion, about forgiving others involved, and about the healing love and forgiveness I now felt from God, enveloped as I was in His expansive embrace. Calvin Miller affirms, "His arms open in a vast, oceanic embrace to enfold me in wonder. It is a splendor that overwhelms me, a glory that engulfs me. It leaves me gawking at the ocean of His love, stupefied by its immensity...."

I was so overwhelmed with wonder at God's grace that I couldn't contain it. I knew it must overflow to others. I knew I must share my story. I drew a deep and nervous breath. "I think I'm finally ready, Lord," I whispered. *You're ready*, came His quiet assurance. I joined the group and, with great fear and faltering, through tears, read my prayers aloud, unveiling the sin I had never revealed. Without a doubt, had I not written in my journal, I never would have found the words or the courage to share. And had I not shared, I never would have seen my listeners' tears. I never would have received their healing embrace, as one by one they came forward to cradle me with compassion; as one by one they empathized with changed hearts, changed minds. Now they understood the devastation abortion wreaks. Had I not shared, I never would have experienced complete release, the weightlessness in my chest, the peace opening up in my heart like a fluttering of wings. I looked out over the ocean, and just then a lone gull rose above the cresting waves on ivory wing. It ascended freely like my unchained soul.

Later that evening, alone on the moonlit beach, I wrote a requiem to Shannon in my journal. Gazing at the sparkling stars, hanging like little lanterns strung across the ocean, I was struck by the truth that abortion has extinguished the lights of millions of lives before they have had their chance to shine. Yet somehow on this clear, crystal night as I searched the heavens, I knew that Shannon and countless children were there with God, illuminating all eternity.

Where is there another God like You Who pardons.... You cannot stay angry at Your people forever, because You delight in showing mercy. Once again You will have compassion on us. You will trample our sins under Your feet and throw them into the depths of the ocean. You will show us Your faithfulness and unfailing love.

MICAH 7:18-20, NLT

Butterfly Blessings

Happiness is a butterfly, which, when pursued, is just beyond our grasp, but which, if you will sit down quietly, may alight upon you.

NATHANIEL HAWTHORNE

I SAT IN THE BUTTERFLY HOUSE, a large glass conservatory that sparkled in the sunlight like a crystal jewel box. Lined with velvet greenery, it was sprinkled with shimmering butterflies, hundreds and hundreds of beautiful butterflies spinning and somersaulting in the air—like a kaleidoscope's colorful stained-glass gems.

Their free-floating gracefulness especially struck me because I *wasn't* free. Still bound to a wheelchair after many months of agonizing pain and swelling from unusual foot surgery complications, I was told by three specialists that I would likely never walk properly or without pain. Depression smothered me. In an effort to cheer me, my husband had suggested this butterfly outing.

Yet joy eluded me. I had hoped to leave the wheelchair in the car, but even the short walk to the conservatory was excruciating. As I sat motionless in my chair, tears stinging my eyes, I knew I was truly losing hope. I feared becoming bitter.

A volunteer's voice interrupted my depressive tailspin. Correcting my husband, she urgently warned, "Sir, please don't touch the butterflies!" Without meaning to disregard the rules, Michael had inadvertently reached up to brush a butterfly in flight. So beautiful, it seemed to beckon an appreciative caress. Yet, even unintentionally, he could have done it great harm. Pablo Picasso cautioned, "If wings of the butterfly are to keep their sheen, you mustn't touch them." Not only would its colorful scales be destroyed, but the butterfly, attempting to escape one's grasp, could sever a leg or wing and ultimately die.

In much the same way, as I grasped for joy and clutched desperately at any little hope for healing, color drained from my life. I thought of a poem by William Blake: "He who binds to himself a joy/ Does the wingèd life destroy;/ But he who kisses the joy as it flies/ Lives in eternity's sunrise." *Kisses the joy as it flies*, I reflected. Despite depressing circumstances, might joy still be flying through my life unnoticed? Certainly it was fluttering by now in a bevy of butterflies—in their dance of delight.

I remembered an earlier visit to the Butterfly House when a lepidopterist advised, "Don't rush at a butterfly. It must come voluntarily; it will land if you sit still." *Sit still.* I pondered those words anew. They seemed sacred now, weighty with wisdom that settled deep in my soul....

My body was still; I had been immobile for month after housebound month, pinned to the hearth-room couch, my injured foot elevated uncomfortably above my heart. But my mind was in a frenzy of fear: Would I ever walk right again? Would I ever be able to stroll

around the block, walk through a super-
market, romp with Sheridan, or even
walk to our postbox to collect the mail
without debilitating pain? Would my
ministry ever be the same? This "foot
ordeal," along with my husband's heart
attack, my father's stroke, my mother's
cancer, and the deaths of several family
members had precluded my writing
and speaking. I had lost precious opportunities. Would God ever use me again?
My heart pounded. My mind raced.
They needed quieting.

Then God's voice calmed me: *Be
still and know that I am God. Be still
and know that I am in control.* George
Seaton Bowes wisely observed, "The
heart that is to be filled to the brim
with holy joy must be held still."
Perhaps that is because when the heart
is still, unencumbered by the "muchness," "manyness," and madness of life,
it is attentive, mindful of blessings, and
receptive to joy. I was beginning to realize that perhaps God had stilled my
body in order to still my mind—in

order that I might become quiet
enough to receive His blessings in the
midst of uncertainty and trial, in order
that the spiritual butterflies of joy and
peace might alight despite my difficult
and unsettling circumstances.

Oh, how I needed to see them! Oh,
how I needed to have them come! I
bowed my head, tears trickling down
my cheeks. *Dear God,* I prayed silently,
please send me a butterfly blessing.

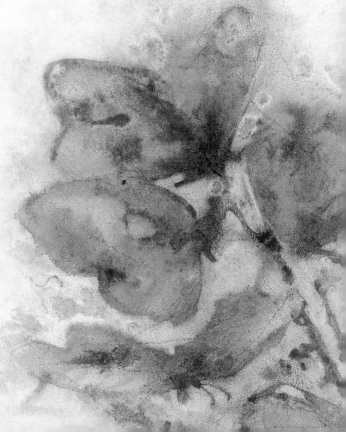

Please let a butterfly descend on me now. It was a prayer of impossibility—one whose fulfillment I thought as elusive as the butterfly I longed to appear. Yet for the first time in months I sensed God's presence—for the first time in months I felt His hope.

I took a deep breath and froze in place, waiting for the impossible, waiting for a moment of wingèd wonder. I sat alone for what seemed an eternity while Michael explored this *papillon* paradise. And then it happened! A butterfly Balanchine performed an airborne ballet just for me, complete with pirouette, arabesque, and *tour jeté*, then took a bow right on my shoulder! I was stunned. It was a hallowed moment. And then he was gone, but not before brushing my cheek with the tip of his wing—a holy kiss, a butterfly blessing, a touch from God.

Michael returned and pushed my wheelchair toward the exit, where I noticed a chrysalis collection in a case on the wall. Though all different in size and shape, they shared one thing: Each was a tomb of transformation, a womb of waiting where the caterpillar must die, in a sense, in order to be born a butterfly. *Will my waiting transform me?* I wondered. *Will my bitterness die in order to birth blessings in my life?*

Cautiously I asked God for more butterfly blessings. Boldly He showered me with a butterfly blizzard! Without my asking, and on days when I needed blessings the most, friends serendipitously sent greeting cards, bookmarks, calendars, a wall plaque, and a gorgeous silk scarf *all* adorned with brilliant butterflies.

As if that weren't enough, God continued to assure me of His presence as I "chanced" upon butterflies in books and poems, on posters and paintings. Many times butterflies appeared unexpectedly in my garden, as I sat in my chair on the deck, and in the middle of the woods at our cabin. Mike even brought me a flaky butterfly pastry I'd been trying for years to locate after our favorite bakery closed. Now I was even *eating* butterflies! Shakespeare proclaimed, "We'll laugh at gilded butterflies." Now I was laughing at glazed ones.

Laughing! How long it had been since I'd laughed. How long it had been since I'd counted my blessings. As I sat still and *noticed*, I realized that blessings abounded and that, to my chagrin, I had ignored them. Blessings had been there all along, amid my trials, amid my testings. I was like the Israelites in Psalm 106, who "did not remember [God's] many kindnesses and they rebelled" (v. 7).

As I considered my blessings, I thought of an anonymous quote I had copied from a fountain in a butterfly garden in Augusta, Missouri: "A butterfly lights beside us like a sunbeam. And for a brief moment, its glory and beauty belong to our world. But then it flies on again, and though we wish it could have stayed, we feel so fortunate to have seen it." I had been so fortunate, but so unaware. I was gifted with glory, but was gathering ashes. How often joy had flitted into my life, but I'd missed it because I was consumed with rebellious complaint rather than resounding thanksgiving.

I realized that all blessings are really butterfly blessings, grace-filled, beautiful, and transitory. I needed a tangible way to appreciate fully these butterfly moments. Luci Shaw speaks of catching truth "securely in the net of words," securely in writing. I suddenly understood that my journal was the butterfly net I needed to capture the reality and memory of my blessings, even after the blessings themselves had flown away. In reading about my butterfly moments, I could still be grateful; I could still be touched by joy.

Robert Louis Stevenson encouraged, "When the clouds gather and rain impends...let us not lose the savor of past mercies and past pleasures; but, like the voice of a bird singing in the rain, let grateful memory survive in the hour of darkness." In times of despair, I don't need to clutch desperately at joy as if it might be lost forever. My journal prayers testify to God's past faithfulness and instill in me fresh hope for the future. They are a way of gratefully remembering—of helping gladness survive.

When I was young, Mother had often repeated another classic Stevenson line: "The world is so full of a number of things, I'm sure we should all be as happy as kings." Daily I began recording my "number of things"—my butterfly blessings of praise and thanksgiving—in what has become my journal of joy.

A blessing that brought me incredible joy is my daughter, Sheridan, herself a butterfly whose childhood has been flitting by with great speed. This prayer captures her essence:

Dear God, thank You for the joy of Sheridan, my beautiful four-year-old imp, who has just interrupted this joyful reverie for the tenth time (honestly!) in fifteen minutes. So much for her quiet time, but I'm maintaining mine. She's a precious, precocious, playful little darling—in addition to being extremely delicate, like fine bone china with roses painted on her cheeks. Thank You for this gift and reward. I don't deserve her. Thank You for entrusting her to me. Thank You for our second ballet class today with Miss Renée. It was sheer joy to see Sheridan flit like a tiny pink butterfly across polished wood floors, plié like a compressing concertina, and instantly relevé, expanding again. Thank You for the grace of dance and the eagerness of young ballerinas—for their graceless grace and lilliputian movements. Thank You for the beauty of tiny proportions.

My love letters to God had expressed my thanksgiving which grew to such great proportions that it overshadowed my pain. In some incomprehensible way, I was thankful *in* my pain, for God had entered into it with me; I was not alone. He drew especially close to me in His Word through what I affectionately dubbed "butterfly verses," those passages that mention safety and refuge under His "wings." His presence was as palpable as the butterfly that had once stroked my cheek.

In *Living with Mystery*, Stacey Padrick comments:

> God *doesn't* remove our suffering or even change our circumstances. He does something greater: *He enters into our suffering with us.* The Lord Jesus enters into the fullness of our pain, here and now, and bears it with us.... If we seek a detour around it, we forfeit a chance to walk alongside the Suffering Servant. In order to know Christ more intimately, to more fully identify with Him, I must share in His sufferings by experiencing suffering myself.

Oh yes, God had entered my suffering, but much more significantly, for the first time *I* had entered His. My foot was pierced like His. *But, my Lord,* I confessed, completely humbled, *it was a scratch, a paper-cut, a surface-wound compared to the torture You endured.* Even a slight sip from His cup of physical suffering had made me profoundly aware and deeply grateful that He had swallowed the bitter brew for me and my sins. Though I had always thanked Jesus for His agonizing death on the cross, now I personally identified with it; I would *never* forget what it had cost Him. I told Him so in a prayer in my journal—I was like the bird singing a praise song in darkness.

And I wanted to share that song with those whom God loves. My wheelchair perspective prompted me to offer kindred-spirit kindness to people I met who were broken in body, broken in heart. I had identified with Christ's suffering, and now I could finally identify with theirs.

C. S. Lewis noted, "Something must drive us out of the nursery to the world of others, and that something is suffering." Though considerate before, now I was compassionate, which means literally *with suffering*. Now I could look into their eyes and know that "empathy is your pain in my heart."

I recalled a wall plaque I'd read in the Butterfly House that incredible day. "Butterflies go wherever they please and please wherever they go." *Lord, make me a butterfly*, I prayed. Now I wanted to *be* a butterfly blessing. Now I wanted to please with compassion those who needed it most—those who needed a touch of His love—those who needed a brush of His wing. The psalmist's words were mine: "For Thou hast been my help, and in the shadow of Thy wings I sing for joy." I could share this joy with others. My chrysalis-turned-crucible experience had changed me because of the redemptive suffering, transforming love, and abundant blessing of Jesus Christ.

Under his wings
you will find refuge.

PSALM 91:4

Faith Blooms

*Faith grows
only in the dark.
You've got to
trust [God]
when you can't
trace Him.*

LYELL RADER

*I*N THE GRAY OF WINTER my family and I
entered a surprisingly deeper darkness, what I've come
to call God's darkroom. Yet as frightening and depressing as it became, I would learn that the blacker the darkroom, the brighter God's glory shines—the more determined the doubt, the deeper the faith that triumphs.

January was a dreary month. My beloved husband, Michael, had almost died of a heart attack, and
my dear great-aunt Martha was dying of cancer. We
had been planning to honor her life with a surprise
eightieth birthday celebration in the near future, but
now she was battling for life itself.

My aunt and I were extremely close. Mart had been like a grandmother to me when my own grandma, her sister Nina, had died years ago. The thought of losing Martha was unbearable. Over and over I had cried out to God in my journal, begging Him to heal her and pleading for the faith to believe He would. Yet my faith, like the ugly amaryllis bulb I'd just planted in a flowerpot on the kitchen windowsill, lay buried beneath ugly fears.

I anguished over Martha's rapidly deteriorating health. Cancer ravaged her body with unrelenting fury, causing her once-supple skin to shrivel tightly over her angular skeleton. Yet somehow the greater her pain and weakness, the greater became her determination to live. Martha had an indomitable spirit, a generous heart, and an inexhaustible capacity for joy—but she wasn't a Christian.

The closer she came to death, the more I feared for her eternal destiny. For years I had prayed for my aunt to recognize Jesus as her Savior and Lord. I scanned old journals and was amazed by the number of times I had asked the Lord to save Aunt Martha, to "translate her from darkness to light." Reading my prayers left me hopeless. I was praying in the darkroom without illumination, and my journals mocked my faith. What was the point of persistent prayer when God hadn't answered? Even now, when Martha was so close to death, she still wasn't interested in God. Worse yet, whenever I talked about Him, she grew uncomfortable, so I usually changed the subject.

Now, with no time to lose, I didn't pray just in my journals; I mustered the courage to pray aloud whenever I was with Martha. Each time she literally pushed me away saying, "Please stop, honey. You're scaring me." Out of respect for her I did stop, but I still sensed God's urgency.

At the hospital, Michael and I met a compassionate chaplain named Jim Grieme, who agreed to visit Martha regularly when she moved to the hospice nursing home. Mart looked forward to his visits and "flirted" with him in her mischievous way, and Jim kept sharing the gospel. Yet whenever Jim mentioned Christ, my aunt grew uneasy. She was especially frightened when he prayed.

One day before I left the nursing home, I told Mart I was going to pray for her. Once more she pushed me away, expressing the fear aroused by my prayers. This time I resolutely remained by her bed, strongly sensing God directing me to ask her why she was afraid. I hesitated. *How can I do that, Lord? She will push me away, and that hurts. I know she isn't personally upset with me, but the thought of prayer makes her miserable.*

God pressed, *How can you not? She will die without Jesus!* Cautiously I obeyed the Lord and asked Martha what frightened her. After a long pause, her anguish spilled out: "I'm afraid of dying!"

At last she had named the terror that gripped her whenever God's name was mentioned. I realized she had equated my prayers with my knowledge of her impending death. I was so relieved to tell her that she didn't need to fear the only One who could help her. With God's enabling, I plainly shared His plan for her salvation—the gift of His Son to pay the penalty for her sins so that she could spend eternity with Him.

A couple days later, Jim visited Mart. As soon as he greeted her, though she was incredibly weak, she countered with, "Oh no. It's you!" Jim knew she was half-joking, but she likely anticipated that he would talk to her again about God. This time as he leaned down by her bed, Mart used all her remaining strength to lift herself up and hug his neck with such force that he dropped to his knees. "I'm so afraid to die," Martha whispered hoarsely in his ear. Jim assured Martha that there was absolutely nothing to fear—that if she knew Christ as her Lord, when she died she would instantly be in heaven with Him. Without coaxing or forcing, Jim simply asked if she wanted Jesus to save her. She said, "Yes," and though her words were barely audible, she repeated Jim's prayer.

The next day when I saw Martha, she tried to hug me, but her arms fell limp by her side. She quietly whispered, "I love you." I sat on her bed for over an hour, stroking her hair and sponging her lips.

Before leaving, I asked Mart if I could pray with her. She nodded. I held her and prayed, and this time she didn't push me away. She was completely peaceful. She smiled sweetly and her eyes radiated joy. I knew beyond doubt that the Holy Spirit now resided in my aunt's heart. I knew she was ready to die—ready to *live!*

When I got home, I felt peace for the first time in weeks. I stopped to linger at the kitchen window, transfixed by the emerald amaryllis shoots now towering two feet over the flowerpot. In the course of less than two months since I'd planted the bulb, I'd watched daily in astonishment at the leaves' skyrocketing growth. I was eager to see the bright red blooms promised by the packaging. In this season of darkness—in the midst of death and doubt—the amaryllis had become to me an undeniable symbol of life and faith. That God could cause such miraculous, beautiful growth from such a hideous-looking bulb had bolstered my belief that He could do the impossible in my aunt's life.

The next day we got the call from my cousin to say Martha had died the previous night shortly after Michael and I left her. I felt lifeless, void, numb. Tears wouldn't come.

The morning of the funeral, as I filled the teakettle at the kitchen sink, I was incredulous. I beheld the impossible—three brilliant crimson blossoms lifted up and opened wide. The amaryllis trumpets had all bloomed! They pointed toward heaven, gloriously heralding the homecoming of my aunt. Those three amazing flowers represented to me the Father, the Son, and the Holy Spirit keeping their promise to welcome Aunt Mart in love. Now my tears flowed—tears of sadness, tears of joy.

In the days following Martha's death, I thought often about God's darkroom and how the Father of Lights sometimes sequesters us in darkness. I realized how light and life paradoxically spring from darkness and death—how silver linings peek around black clouds, butterflies flutter from chrysalises, amaryllises spring from dirt-covered bulbs, and photographic images emerge in darkrooms.

During the dark and fear-filled night of Martha's soul—during her time in God's darkroom—God's glory had shone the brightest. It was there that He did His best work, using the worst trial of my aunt's life to develop the film of faith in her heart, transferring the image of His Son onto hers. I had prayed for God to heal Mart's body, but He did something even more miraculous: He healed her soul!

Although Aunt Martha had endured one of the longest, most excruciating deaths possible, God used her suffering to cause her to reach out to Him when she might not have otherwise. Her suffering was a "momentary, light affliction" compared with the eternal joy she was now experiencing in heaven—the biggest celebration imaginable!

And I had the joy of knowing that despite my wavering belief, God had done the impossible, bringing life out of death and faith out of doubt—growing faith in my aunt's darkness and in mine. I reread my journals once more in the light—in the light of God's faithfulness, in the light of Aunt Martha's astounding salvation. This time I read between the lines of my prayers. Though I hadn't been able to trace God's work developing in the darkness, now I could see the evidence of His transforming touch in the light.

With God all things are possible.

MATTHEW 19:26

God's Patchwork, My Passion

I make [quilts] warm to keep my family from freezing; I make them beautiful to keep my heart from breaking.

A PRAIRIE WOMAN IN 1870

*O*H, GOD! I DON'T BELIEVE I ACTUALLY TOLD HER NO! *I must be crazy. You know I've wanted this job most of my professional career!* I anguished as I drove home from the interview that frigid February day. My mentor and friend Sally Howell had offered me my dream job as her assistant; together we'd supervise a large hospital volunteer program. It was a job for which I had longed, prayed, and applied repeatedly at other hospitals, but it had eluded me for sixteen years. Now Sally had offered it, and unbelievably I had declined.

Four years earlier I had left a full-time career in order to raise my baby daughter. I dearly loved Sheridan, and yet, without employment for the first time in twenty years, I had experienced times of doubt, depression, and disorientation. Sheridan would be in kindergarten soon. What would I do then? What was my purpose—my passion— my place in life's "pattern" beyond my calling as a mother?

When Sally made the offer, one I had not solicited, I presumed this was God's cue for me to reenter the job market. What a blessing to be offered a position that matched my professional skills and dreams; yet I couldn't say yes. The hours would have consumed precious time best spent with Sheridan, and the salary wouldn't cover child-care costs. Why had God allowed my dream, this new-career carrot, to be temptingly dangled in front of me? It seemed like a cruel tease....

Nothing made sense. Disappointment became bewilderment, then numbness. I felt as void and lifeless as the white sky above me and frozen roadway before me. *Where is joy?* I wondered. *Lord, when will I sing again?*

Immediately, God encouraged me. Looking up, I noticed telephone wires suspended across the highway like a musical staff. Birds at various levels punctuated the lines like little black notes. As I sped by, insulated by my car's closed windows, I couldn't hear them, but I knew they were singing. Reassured, I remembered the psalmist's words: "Sing to the Lord a new song."

In *Shattered Dreams*, Larry Crabb elaborates, "God is always working to make His children aware of a dream that remains alive beneath the rubble of every shattered dream, a new dream that when realized will release a new song, sung with tears, till God wipes them away and we sing with nothing but joy in our hearts." I knew that even though it seemed impossible, God would somehow bring something good from this disappointment, that He would give me a new dream, a new hope, a new song.

Arriving home, I brewed a cup of tea, lit a fire, and opened the cedar chest to get a throw. Needing extra comfort, I fingered through the heavy pile of blankets until I felt my beloved old patchwork quilt. I rarely used it because it was threadbare, as worn as the loving hands that had painstakingly fashioned it.

I could still see the parchment-crinkled hands of my great-grandmother, Enola "MaMa" Ayers—hands that could animate conversation with sweeping gestures or guide a needle with a surgeon's precision. MaMa cut each scrap for her quilts from her colorful dresses, from her colorful life. At times the pieces unraveled, and she sutured them together with the same love that had stayed my childhood fears and mended my heart into wholeness.

My heart needed mending now, much as MaMa's had so many years before. She said that quilting had saved her sanity. When she was a child, she helped her mother quilt to protect the family from the winter's cold blasts. When she was an adult, she quilted to protect her heart from the world's cruel blows. When MaMa was eighty-one, a serious fall and broken hip left her virtually housebound; she nearly died of pneumonia and never walked well again. Most of her friends had died, and she felt alone, broken, and useless—without a dream, without a hope, without a song.

To occupy her time and mind, she

made a quilt for her son's wedding anniversary; it became the first of many. Before she died at ninety-seven, MaMa's quilting pastime had become her quintessential purpose; she was pursuing her new dream of leaving a legacy of love for her grandchildren and great-grandchildren. Although legally blind, she *hand-stitched* over twenty-five patchwork quilts, one for every member of her family. She allowed God to sew a pattern for good from the shreds of her despair—to stitch beauty from the scraps of her life. MaMa always hummed a little tune when she quilted. I know it was the song of joy.

On this bleak February day, I felt close to MaMa and her dream as I retrieved my treasured quilt. Gingerly lifting it from the chest, I discovered a box beneath its folds. Opening the lid, I unearthed more treasures, long ago misplaced and since forgotten. Its contents were a crazy quilt cut from the fabric of my life—a patchwork potpourri of my school photos, drawings, report cards, book reports, poems, letters, childhood writings, and high-school journals.

As I spread the papers before me, I was surprised to see an unmistakable pattern emerge—my love and gift for language. I paused to read teachers' encouraging comments. The capstone was Miss Fisher's inscription on my French poem: "Extremely beautiful in French as in English. Very well done. Would you permit me to publish it in the school newspaper?" I had completely forgotten her remarks and suggestions for publication.

I began thumbing through my old journals, repeatedly reading about how I had enjoyed my writing assignments. I had even mentioned my desire to write a sixth-grade girls magazine with my best friend. Excitedly I realized that I was tracing a pattern of God's design for my life.

This nostalgic journey, courtesy of words I'd written long ago, helped me appreciate what author Robert Benson remarked about his journals:

The collection of pages will show you a pattern and give you clues as to what must be done and what must be let go. It will teach you how far you have come and how far you must go, and the source of your strength for the travels ahead.... Your own story begins to take shape in these pages, the tale of your own life along the Road Home. The threads of it, and its colors and textures, begin to reveal the ways of God in the Way that you travel. You begin to get a glimpse here and there of who you really are.

I was beginning to see who I really was. These youthful writing remnants and journal jottings, though rough and ragged around the edges, were the missing pieces of my "purpose pattern"—a tatterdemalion testament of a dream slowly shaping, a dream to write.

But how could this be? I had been a vocal major, who never took a single college English class. After graduation, though I didn't teach music, I dreamed of performing. That dream never materialized. I dabbled in secretarial work, office management, and nonprofit administration. Now my dream of hospital volunteer administration was over. Why had these dreams died, and why had I never pursued professional writing?

Larry Crabb says:

When lesser dreams reliably come true, we have a hard time appreciating greater dreams. We neither envision nor pursue them.... When good dreams shatter, better ones are there newly to value and pursue. These better dreams are indestructible; they will not be taken away from us either by God (because He is good) or by the forces of hell (because evil has no power to thwart God's highest purposes). No matter what happens in life, a wonderful dream is available, always, that if pursued will generate an unfamiliar, radically new internal perspective. That experience, though strange at first, will eventually be recognized as joy.

I believe George Eliot's wisdom: "It is never too late to become what you might have been." So that night, with much trepidation, I wrote a prayer of submission in my journal, accepting God's plan. Although I loved writing and felt this dream was God's will, I still felt uncomfortable in my would-be-published writer's skin. I struggled to let go of the old dreams, the old desires, the old delights. It was difficult to move forward.

The "Road Home," as Benson calls it, to being who I am has not been a simple stroll around the block while whistling a happy tune. My road to publication has been paved with difficulties.

I've sung my share of doleful descants. One pays a price for passion. There are sacrifices of time, camaraderie, interests, and resources. There are painful rejections and frustrating instances of one's commitment being misunderstood. At times I have wanted to deny my dream. But as one passionate writer expressed it, "In denying the dream we deny the work the Holy Spirit would do with it in others' lives. If we do not dream the melody, the ears that wait will not hear the music that will set them free. For our song is never intended for our ears alone, but to give grace and music and a new song to all who hear."

Oswald Chambers wrote, "Beware of harking back to what you were once when God wants you to be something you have never been." I believe that when God let my old desires die, He was doing a new thing, a good thing, a better thing. He was ripping apart my unmet dreams by the seams so that He could rearrange them into a pattern that fit His good purposes—a pattern of passion that would strangely warm my heart with joy, that would enable me to share His love and hope with others.

Moreover we know that
to those who love God,
who are called according to His plan,
everything that happens
fits into a pattern for good.

ROMANS 8:28, PHILLIPS

Take the Plunge!

WHEN SHE WAS SIX, Sheridan would freeze before jumping into deep water. "Don't be afraid, Sheridan," her swimming teacher, would encourage. "It's just like being in shallow water. The water will hold you up!"

When you're a new swimmer, jumping into deep water can be absolutely terrifying. You just know you will either drown or, at best, flail around in water over your head, gulping, gasping, and grabbing for life. But if you relax, breathe deeply, and stop fighting, you'll float and discover that the water is your ally; it will indeed hold you up.

If you don't think you write well, jumping into your prayer journal can feel just as intimidating as diving into deep water does for a beginning swimmer. Taking the plunge can be risky. You may fear you will drown in a whirlpool of unexplored emotions. You may dread thrashing about in an undertow of incoherent thoughts, misspelled words, grammatical errors, or simplistic vocabulary. You may think it's futile to splash around nervously on the page, getting nowhere fast.

Don't be afraid. Jump in *now* and write to God about wherever you are in life. Get your pen wet, and let your thoughts flow freely from your head to your heart to your hand and onto the page. Remember that God is a writer and that you, made in His image, are a writer too! Be encouraged! Because God has created language, He can give you words with which to pray about your feelings, fears, sins, mistakes, questions, joys, praises, passions—words that will draw you close to Him, words that He will not correct like a term paper but will cherish for their heartfelt sincerity. He loves you and will treasure whatever you write.

*It is never static. This creek is
like my stream of consciousness.
Its flow is so like my own
living or writing—slow, and reflectively
lazy, sometimes,
or full and fierce in the
rush of ideas and work.
It is my metaphor—
intensely personal.
I am writing a stream.
I am living a creek.*

LUCI SHAW

So take the plunge. Dive in. It's safe. You won't drown. The water of words will hold you up. You won't need to grope for them because the current of God's Spirit will gently move you along to wherever He wants you to go—whether to write a little or whether to write a lot.

Remember that "the deep waters of the Holy Spirit are always accessible, because they are always *proceeding*." The Old Testament prophet Ezekiel saw a vision of such "proceeding" water trickling from under the temple door. In Ezekiel 47, a man measured the water, which was at first ankle-deep. It rose to knee-deep and then to waist-deep. Before it reached the Dead Sea, it was a full-flowing river. Amazingly, when the river emptied into the sea, the saltwater became fresh. The man said, "When [the river] reaches the sea, its waters are healed.... There will be a very great multitude of fish, because these waters go there; for they will be healed, and everything will live wherever the river goes" (vv. 8-9, NKJV). This miraculous river changed a sea of death into a sea of life.

Similarly, when God guides our prayer writing—and He does—we float on streams of living water that bring healing to our soul. We are always moving into life because when God moves us into the deep waters of prayer, we will always catch "fish." As we take the plunge and flow along with the words, we'll catch marvelous new insights with our pens, insights that feed our souls and strengthen our hearts.

What God enables to flow will be unique for each person and circumstance. For me, writing my prayers is sometimes like swirling in a raging emotional river. But more often, it is like floating on a mellow, meandering thought-stream. God leads me gently, one petition, one praise, one confession at a time. Yet each of us must start somewhere. The easiest thing to do is to abandon fear, take the risk, jump straight into your journal, and simply let your thoughts flow. The water is fine. You can trust God; He won't let you drown.

Elisabeth Elliot tells the story of her little brother, Dave, who was terrified to jump into the ocean, though their father was prepared to catch him. "Dave was sure it would mean certain disaster, and he could not trust his father." Finally, on the last day of vacation, he got up nerve and took the plunge straight into his dad's waiting arms. He had so much fun that he burst into tears and howled, "Why didn't you *make* me go in?"

No one can make you jump into your prayer journal—into the deep waters of your soul. But when you do, rest assured that God will catch you. I suspect before long you will joyfully exclaim, "Lord, what took me so long?"

Put out into deep water, and let down the nets for a catch.

LUKE 5:4

Love Letters to God

"Fullness of joy"—Psalm 16:11.

"Love always wants to proclaim itself"—Michelle Lovric, *How to Write Love Letters* (New York: Shooting Star Press, 1995), 7.

"My heart is overflowing"—Psalm 45:1, TLB.

Love letters are "our heart on our sleeve"—Lovric, *How to Write Love Letters*, 5.

"Golden bowls of heaven"—Revelation 5:8.

Secret Garden of the Soul

Emilie Barnes—Emilie Barnes, *Time Began in a Garden* (Eugene, Oreg.: Harvest House, 1995), 9.

Dorothy Frances Gurney—Dorothy Frances Gurney, "God's Garden," in Hazel Felleman, comp., *The Best Loved Poems of the American People* (Garden City, N.Y.: Doubleday & Co., 1936), 137.

"In the secret place"—Matthew 6:6, NKJV.

Jesus prayed...in "lonely places"—Luke 5:16.

Gordon MacDonald—Gordon MacDonald, *Ordering Your Private World* (Nashville, Tenn.: Oliver Nelson, 1985), 126-7.

Ibid., 136.

Thomas R. Kelly—Thomas R. Kelly, *A Testament of Devotion* (New York: Harper San Francisco, 1992), 92.

"We are considerably poorer"—Leslie Williams, *Night Wrestling* (Dallas, Tex.: Word, 1997), 137.

"Love is the fairest bloom"—Anonymous.

We should be anxious for nothing—Philippians 4:6.

Bye-Bye Blackbird!

"Pack up all my care and woe"—Mort Dixon, "Bye-Bye Blackbird" (Jerome H. Remick & Co., 1926).

Jesus tells us repeatedly not to worry—Matthew 6:25-34.

"I am my lover's and my lover is mine"— Song of Songs 6:3.

"All at once, my life [took] sudden shape"—Anne Morrow Lindbergh, "Flight of the Birds," *The Unicorn and Other Poems* (New York: Pantheon Books, 1956), 64.

"snippet from quote"—As quoted in Ewald M. Plass, comp., *What Luther Says: An Anthology*, vol. 3 (St. Louis, Mo.: Concordia Publishing House, 1959), 1344.

Lists of Lament

"Record my lament"—Psalm 56:8.

That "inner silent wail"—Elisabeth Elliot, *Secure in the Everlasting Arms* (Ann Arbor, Mich.: Servant Publications, 2002), 49-50.

Shakespeare—Shakespeare, *Macbeth*, 5.1.50-5.

Elizabeth Barrett Browning—Elizabeth Barrett Browning, "De Profundis," stanza 21, in John Bartlett, *Familiar Quotations* (Boston, Mass.: Little, Brown and Company, 1980), 507:24.

"My tears declared"—Timothy Jones, *Awake My Soul* (New York: Doubleday, 1999), 186.

Edwin Markham—Edwin Markham in Draper, *Draper's Book of Quotations for the Christian World*, 141, #2508.

I Only Have Eyes for You

"Sweet little Jesus boy"—Robert MacGimsey, *Sweet Little Jesus Boy*, Carl Fischer, New York, NY, 1934.

A. W. Tozer—A. W. Tozer, *The Pursuit of God* (Camp Hill, Penn.: Christian Publications, 1993), 30.

Anne Morrow Lindbergh—Anne Morrow Lindbergh, *Gift from the Sea* (New York: Pantheon Books, 1955), 114.

Richard Baxter—Richard Baxter in Draper, *Draper's Book of Quotations for the Christian World*, 572, #10425.

Leslie Williams, *Seduction of the Lesser Gods* (Nashville, Tenn.: Word Publishing, 1997), 13.

"Looking unto Jesus"—Theodore Monod, as quoted by Anne Ortlund, *I Want to See You, Lord* (Eugene, Oreg.: Harvest House Publishers, 1998), 108.

Letting Go

Elisabeth Elliot—Elisabeth Elliot, *Secure in the Everlasting Arms*, 39.

Luci Shaw—Luci Shaw, *LifePath* (Portland, Oreg.: Multnomah Publishers, 1991), 80-1.

A. W. Tozer—A. W. Tozer in Edythe Draper, comp., *Draper's Book of Quotations for the Christian World* (Wheaton, Ill.: Tyndale, 1992), 255, #4733.

"I also knew that trees don't sin by complaining"—Lynn D. Morrissey, Adapted from *Seasons of a Woman's Heart* (Lancaster, Penn.: Starburst Publishers, 1999), 61.

Luci Shaw—Shaw, *LifePath*, 99.

Oceans of Mercy, Oceans of Love

Post-Abortion Society —"Post-Abortion Society" was coined by Carol Everett in *Blood Money* (Portland, Oreg.: Multnomah Publishers, 1992).

Drinking wine was "dissipation"—Ephesians 5:18.

C. S. Lewis—C. S. Lewis, in Draper, *Draper's Book of Quotations for the Christian World*, 220, #4087.

Calvin Miller—Calvin Miller, *Jesus Loves Me* (New York: Warner Books, 2002), 20.

"Bethesda Pool's paralytic"— see John 5:1-15.

Butterfly Blessings

William Blake—William Blake, "Several Questions Answered," in John Bartlett, *Familiar Quotations* (Boston, Mass.: Little, Brown and Company, 1980), 404:18.

George Seaton Bowes —George Seaton Bowes, *QuoteWorld.org*, www.quoteworld.org/author.php?thetext =George+Seaton+Bowes (accessed 18 July 2003).

Muchness and *manyness*— Richard Foster coined the words *muchness* and *manyness*.

Luci Shaw—*Life Path*, p. 88

Robert Louis Stevenson— Robert Louis Stevenson, as quoted in Jane Rubietta, *Still Waters* (Minneapolis, Minn.: Bethany House, 1999), 130.

"The world is so full of a number of things"—Robert Louis Stevenson, "Happy Thought," *A Child's Garden of Verses* (San Francisco, Calif.: Chronicle Books, 1989), 44.

Stacey Padrick—Stacey Padrick, *Living with Mystery* (Minneapolis, Minn.: Bethany House, 2001), 94-5.

C. S. Lewis—C. S. Lewis as quoted by Brenda Waggoner in *The Velveteen Woman* (Colorado Springs, CO: Chariot Victor Publishing, 1999), 184.

"Empathy is your pain in my heart"—Halford E. Luccock, Draper, p. 170, #3068.

"Butterflies go wherever they please..."—Anonymous.

"For Thou hast been my help"—Psalm 63:7.

Faith Blooms

"Translate her from darkness to light"—see Collossians 1:13, KJV

"Momentary, light affliction" —2 Corinthians 4:17, NASB.

God's Patchwork, My Passion

"Sing to the Lord a new song"—Psalm 96:1a.

Larry Crabb—Larry Crabb, *Shattered Dreams*, Colorado Springs, Col.: WaterBrook Press, 2001), 82.

"The parchment-crinkled hands of my great-grandmother" —Lynn D. Morrissey, adapted from *Treasures of a Woman's Heart* (Lancaster, Penn.: Starburst, 2000), vii.

Robert Benson—Robert Benson, *Living Prayer* (New York: Jeremy P. Tarcher/Putnam, a member of Penguin Putnam, Inc., 1998), 180.

Larry Crabb—Larry Crabb *Shattered Dreams*, 53.

George Eliot—George Eliot *The Harvard Extension School Alumni Bulletin*, www.dce.harvard.edu/pubs/alum/1996/fall/3.html.

"In denying the dream" —Jane Rubietta, *Quiet Places* (Minneapolis, Minn.: Bethany House, 1997), 140.

Oswald Chambers—Oswald Chambers, *My Utmost for His Highest* (Westwood, N.J.: Barbour and Company, Inc., 1963), 160.

Take the Plunge!

"The deep waters of the Holy Spirit"—Mrs. Charles E. Cowman, *Streams in the Desert* (Uhrichsville, Ohio: Barbour Publishing, Inc., 1928), Day 2/29.

Elisabeth Elliot—Elisabeth Elliot, *Keep a Quiet Heart* (Ann Arbor, Mich.: Servant Publications, 1995), 32.

Acknowledgments

Thank You, Lord, for loving, saving, and forgiving me. It amazes me that You would use me. I am a prodigal whom You have treated like a princess.

With deep gratitude for their inestimable contributions:

Anne Ortlund and Becky Tirabassi for their books,
which encouraged me to keep writing my prayers.

My Lifeliner and SOS prayer partners; the delightful Deborah Circle and friends
at Central Presbyterian Church, for continually praying about my writing.
There would literally be no book without you!

The Multnomah publishing team, for their belief against all odds in the life-changing message of
this book: Don Jacobson, for giving me the chance of a lifetime; Lisa Stilwell, for her artistic
excellence in casting a creative vision so far-reaching and remarkable that it still takes my breath
away; Lisa Guest, for carefully holding a tuning fork to my work and, with perfect-pitch precision,
fine-tuning it with grace and ease; Jennifer Gott, Brian Thomasson, Sandy Muller, Gayle Vickery,
Multnomah sales representatives, and everyone else who worked tirelessly behind the scenes to
ensure excellence—though I may never meet you, I will always appreciate you.

Judy Gordon, for her amazing compassion, journaling passion,
belief in my writing, and incredible assistance in opening the door.

My Journal Joggers, who jogged alongside to encourage with their invaluable writing critiques:
Gail Boutelle, Jan Buckman, Joan Clayton, Gayle DeSalles, Pat Devine, Jo Doolittle, Sylvia Duncan,
Marilyn Gosh, Pat Knox, Jo Manwarren, Susan Reis, Suz Ryan, and Becky & Bill Steinmeier.

Michael, my beloved husband, friend, and Renaissance man, for believing,
editing, encouraging, cooking, cleaning, teasing, and prodding—*anything* to keep me
on track to completion. Darling, now that the book is written, does this mean I'll have to
learn to cook and—worse yet—to do it?! I love you!

Sheridan, my darling daughter, for her sweet support in giving Mama writing room,
tea-party breaks, and tender hugs. I love you, Budgie!

Bill Morrissey, for his persistent yet good-natured pushing. See, Daddy, it paid off!
I finally wrote a solo book. So there!

Donna Norman, for her abiding love and belief in my dream for more years than we can count.
From Bach to Bible studies to books to birthdays, we've shared it all, sweetie!

Jo Manwarren, for her blessed friendship, daily prayers, "business lunch" phone breaks,
and "mission impossible" challenges. Not one phone booth blew up, Jo!

Armené Humber, for tenderly cupping my vision and fanning the flame.

Florence Littauer, for her personal challenge for excellence in writing, speaking, and living.

Becky Freeman, for extending a lifeline of hope when I was ready to quit.

JoAnn Hanes, and Joanie and Al McNair for their precious prayers and notes of encouragement.

Bill Steinmeier, Shirley Ann Ross, Sally Howell, Jo Doolittle, and Jackie Mullins,
for seeing a writing gift that I couldn't.

Brad Werner, for his gracious encouragement and theological insights.

Jan Buchman, Jennifer Kennedy Dean, Dan Doriani, Bill Jensen, Carol Kent,
Jo Manwarren, Kathy Collard Miller, Donna Norman, Karen O'Connor, Jessica Shaver,
Betty and Bill Steinmeir, Lisa Stilwell, George Stulac, and Lysa TerKeurst,
for their compassion and discernment about the "Oceans" essay.